Your Little Catechism

Your fabulous journey with God is just beginning. Along the way you will have many questions. Questions are good. God places questions in your heart and mind for many different reasons. Follow your questions, wherever they might lead you.

Some of your questions will be easy to find answers to. To help us answer many of our questions, our spiritual leaders have given us the *Catechism of the Catholic Church*. The answers we find there have been revealed by God and by nature over the centuries.

In the pages that follow we will share with you some questions you may have about God and life. The answers are easy to read but often hard to live. But the answers will help you become the-best-version-of-yourself, grow in virtue, and live a holy life.

There will be other times in your life when you have questions that cannot be answered by words on a page, such as what vocation you are called to or what career you should pursue. At these times you will seek deeply personal answers to deeply personal questions.

These questions require a lot more patience. Seek the advice of wise people who love the Lord. Read what wise men and women before you have had to say on such topics. But, most of all, pray and ask God to show you his way.

As you make this journey you will encounter others who have questions. Help them as best you can to find the answers. People deserve answers to their questions.

And never, ever, forget . . . you are blessed!

My name is

_____

I am blessed, and God made me wonderfully and marvelously in his own image. Jesus wants me to become the-best-version-of-myself, grow in virtue, and live a holy life.

1. **Q: Who made you?**

   A: God made you.

   In the Bible: Genesis 1:1, 26–27; Genesis 2:7, 21–22
   In the *Catechism*: *CCC*, 355

2. **Q: Does God love you?**

   A: Yes. God loves you more than anyone in the world,
   and more than you could ever imagine.

   In the Bible: John 3:16
   In the *Catechism*: *CCC*, 457, 458

3. **Q: Why did God make you?**

   A: God made you to know him, love him, to carry out the mission he
   entrusts to you in this world, and to be happy with him forever in
   heaven.

   In the Bible: Deuteronomy 10:12–15; John 17:3
   In the *Catechism*: *CCC*, 1, 358

4. Q: What is God?

A: God is an infinite and perfect spirit.

In the Bible: Exodus 3:6; Isaiah 44:6; 1 John 4:8, 16
In the *Catechism*: *CCC*, 198–200, 212, 221

5. Q: Did God have a beginning?

A: No. God has no beginning. He always was and he always will be.

In the Bible: Psalm 90:2; Revelation 1:8
In the *Catechism*: *CCC*, 202

6. Q: Where is God?

A: Everywhere.

In the Bible: Psalm 139
In the *Catechism*: *CCC*, 1

7. Q: Does God see us?

A: God sees us and watches over us.

In the Bible: Wisdom 11:24–26; Jeremiah 1:5
In the *Catechism*: *CCC*, 37, 301, 302

8. **Q: Does God know everything?**

A: Yes. God knows all things, even our most secret thoughts, words, and actions.

In the Bible: Job 21:22; Psalm 33:13–15; Psalm 147:4–5
In the *Catechism*: CCC, 208

9. **Q: Is God all loving, just, holy, and merciful?**

A: Yes, God is all loving, all just, all holy, and all merciful—and he invites us to be loving, just, holy, and merciful too.

In the Bible: John 13:34; 1 John 4:8; Ephesians 2:4
In the *Catechism*: CCC, 214, 211, 208

10. **Q: Is there only one God?**

A: Yes, there is only one God.

In the Bible: Isaiah 44:6; John 8:58
In the *Catechism*: CCC, 253

11. **Q: Why is there only one God?**

A: There can only be one God, because God, being supreme and infinite, cannot have an equal.

In the Bible: Mark 12:29–30
In the *Catechism*: *CCC*, 202

12. **Q: How many Persons are there in God?**

A: In God there are three divine Persons, unique and distinct and yet equal in all things—the Father, the Son, and the Holy Spirit.

In the Bible: 1 Corinthians 12:4–6; 2 Corinthians 13:13; Ephesians 4:4–6
In the *Catechism*: *CCC*, 252, 254, 255

13. **Q: Is the Father God?**

A: Yes.

In the Bible: Exodus 3:6; Exodus 4:22
In the *Catechism*: *CCC*, 253, 262

14. **Q: Is the Son God?**

    A: Yes.

    > In the Bible: John 8:58; John 10:30
    > In the *Catechism*: CCC, 253, 262

15. **Q: Is the Holy Spirit God?**

    A: Yes.

    > In the Bible: John 14:26; John 15:26
    > In the *Catechism*: CCC, 253, 263

16. **Q: What is the Holy Trinity?**

    A: The Holy Trinity is one God in three divine Persons—Father, Son, and Holy Spirit.

    > In the Bible: Matthew 28:19
    > In the *Catechism*: CCC, 249, 251

17. **Q. What is free will?**

    A: Free will is an incredible gift from God that allows us to make our own decisions. This incredible gift comes with incredible responsibility.

    In the Bible: Sirach 15:14–15
    In the *Catechism*: *CCC*, 1731

18. **Q. What is sin?**

    A: Sin is any willful thought, word, deed, or omission contrary to the law of God.

    In the Bible: Genesis 3:5; Exodus 20:1–17
    In the *Catechism*: *CCC*, 1850

19. **Q: How many kinds of sin are there?**

    A: There are two actual kinds of sin—venial and mortal.

    In the Bible: 1 John 5:16–17
    In the *Catechism*: *CCC*, 1855

20. Q: **What is a venial sin?**

A: A venial sin is a slight offense against God.

In the Bible: Matthew 5:19; Matthew 12:32; 1 John 5:16–18
In the *Catechism: CCC*, 1855, 1863

21. Q: **What is a mortal sin?**

A: A mortal sin is a grievous offense against God and his law.

In the Bible: Matthew 12:32; 1 John 5:16–18
In the *Catechism: CCC*, 1855, 1857

22. Q: **Does God abandon us when we sin?**

A: Never. God is always calling to us, pleading with us, to return to him
and his ways.

In the Bible: Psalm 103: 9–10, 13; Jeremiah 3:22; Matthew 28:20; Luke 15:11–32
In the *Catechism: CCC*, 27, 55, 982

23. Q: Which Person of the Holy Trinity became man?

A: The Second Person, God the Son, became man without giving up his divine nature.

In the Bible: 1 John 4:2
In the *Catechism*: *CCC*, 423, 464

24. Q: What name was given to the Second Person of the Holy Trinity when he became man?

A: Jesus.

In the Bible: Luke 1:31; Matthew 1:21
In the *Catechism*: *CCC*, 430

25. Q: When the Son became man, did he have a human mother?

A: Yes.

In the Bible: Luke 1:26–27
In the *Catechism*: *CCC*, 488, 490, 495

26. **Q: Who was Jesus' mother?**
    A: The Blessed Virgin Mary.

    > In the Bible: Luke 1:30, 31; Matthew 1:21–23
    > In the *Catechism*: *CCC*, 488, 495

27. **Q: Why do we honor Mary?**
    A: Because she is the mother of Jesus and our mother too.

    > In the Bible: Luke 1:48; John 19:27
    > In the *Catechism*: *CCC*, 971

28. **Q: Who was Jesus' real father?**
    A: God the Father.

    > In the Bible: Luke 1:35; John 17:1
    > In the *Catechism*: *CCC*, 422, 426, 442

29. **Q: Who was Jesus' foster father?**

A: Joseph.

> In the Bible: Matthew 1:19, 20; Matthew 2:13, 19—21
> In the *Catechism*: CCC, 437, 488, 1655

30. **Q: Is Jesus God, or is he man, or is he both God and man?**

A: Jesus is both God and man; as the Second Person of the Holy Trinity, he is God; and since he took on a human nature from his mother Mary, he is man.

> In the Bible: Philippians 2:6—7; John 1:14, 16; John 13:3; 1 John 4:2
> In the *Catechism*: CCC, 464, 469

31. **Q: Was Jesus also a man?**

A: Yes, Jesus was fully God and fully human.

> In the Bible: Luke 24:39; 1 John 4:2—3
> In the *Catechism*: CCC, 464, 469, 470

32. **Q: On what day was Jesus born?**

A: Jesus was born on Christmas day in a stable in Bethlehem.

In the Bible: Luke 2:1–20; Matthew 1:18–25
In the *Catechism*: CCC, 437, 563

33. **Q: What is the Incarnation?**

A: The Incarnation is the belief that Jesus became man.

In the Bible: John 1:14; 1 John 4:2
In the *Catechism*: CCC, 461, 463

34. **Q: Did Jesus love life?**

A: Yes.

In the Bible: John 10:10; John 2:1–12
In the *Catechism*: CCC, 221, 257, 989

35. Q: If Jesus loved life why did he willingly die on the cross?

A: He died on the cross because he loved you and me even more than life.

In the Bible: Romans 5:8; John 15:13; Ephesians 5:2
In the *Catechism*: CCC, 1825, 604

36. Q: Why did Jesus suffer and die?

A: So that we could be forgiven our sins, and live with him in heaven forever after this life.

In the Bible: John 3:16; 2 Corinthians 5:14–16
In the *Catechism*: CCC, 604, 618, 620

37. Q: What do we call the mystery of God becoming man?

A: The mystery of the Incarnation.

In the Bible: John 1:14; 1 John 4:2
In the *Catechism*: CCC, 461, 463

38. **Q: On what day did Jesus die on the cross?**

A: Good Friday, the day after the Last Supper.

> In the Bible: John 19:16–40; Matthew 27:33–50
> In the *Catechism: CCC*, 641

39. **Q: On what day did Jesus rise from the dead?**

A: On Easter Sunday, three days after Good Friday.

> In the Bible: Matthew 28:1–6; Mark 16:1–8
> In the *Catechism: CCC*, 1169, 1170

40. **Q: What gifts do we receive as a result of being saved by Jesus?**

A: By dying on the cross Jesus restored our relationship with God and opened a floodgate of grace.

> In the Bible: Luke 23:44–46; Romans 3:21–26; 2 Corinthians 5:17–21
> In the *Catechism: CCC*, 1026, 1047

41. Q: What is grace?

A: Grace is the help God gives us to respond generously to his call, to do what is good and right, grow in virtue, and live holy lives.

In the Bible: John 1:12–18; 2 Corinthians 12:9
In the *Catechism*: CCC, 1996

42. Q: What is faith?

A: Faith is a gift from God. It is a supernatural virtue that allows us to firmly believe all the truth that God has revealed to us.

In the Bible: Hebrews 11:1
In the *Catechism*: CCC, 1814

43. Q: What is hope?

A: Hope is a gift from God. It is a supernatural virtue that allows us to firmly trust that God will keep all his promises and lead us to heaven.

In the Bible: Romans 8:24–25; 1 Timothy 4:10; 1 Timothy 1:1; Hebrews 6:18–20
In the *Catechism*: CCC, 1817, 1820–1821

44. **Q: What is charity?**

A: Charity is a gift from God. It is a supernatural virtue that allows us to love God above everything else, and our neighbor as ourselves.

In the Bible: John 13:34; 1 Corinthians 13:4–13
In the *Catechism*: *CCC*, 1822, 1823, 1825

45. **Q: Will God give you the gifts of faith, hope, and charity?**

A: Yes, God gives the gifts of faith, hope, and charity, freely to all those who ask for them sincerely and consistently.

In the Bible: 1 Corinthians 13:13
In the *Catechism*: *CCC*, 1813

46. **Q: How long will God love me for?**

A: God will love you forever.

In the Bible: John 13:1; Romans 8:35–39
In the *Catechism*: *CCC*, 219

47. **Q: When did Jesus ascend into heaven?**

A: On Ascension Thursday, forty days after Easter.

> In the Bible: Acts 1:9; Mark 16:19
> In the *Catechism: CCC,* 659

48. **Q: When did the Holy Spirit descend upon the apostles?**

A: On Pentecost Sunday, fifty days after Easter.

> In the Bible: John 20:21–22; Matthew 28:19
> In the *Catechism: CCC,* 731, 1302

49. **Q: What is meant by the Redemption?**

A: Redemption means that Jesus' Incarnation, life, death, and Resurrection paid the price for our sins, opened the gates of heaven, and freed us from slavery to sin and death.

> In the Bible: Ephesians 1:7; Romans 4:25
> In the *Catechism: CCC,* 517, 606, 613

50. **Q: What did Jesus establish to continue his mission of Redemption?**

A: He established the Catholic Church.

In the Bible: Matthew 16:18
In the *Catechism*: *CCC*, 773, 778, 817, 822

51. **Q: Why do we believe that the Catholic Church is the one true church?**

A: Because it is the only church established by Jesus.

In the Bible: Matthew 16:18
In the *Catechism*: *CCC*, 750

52. **Q: Does it matter to which church or religion you belong?**

A: Yes, in order to be faithful to Jesus, it is necessary to remain in the church he established.

In the Bible: Mark 16:16; John 3:5
In the *Catechism*: *CCC*, 846

53. **Q: What are the four marks of the Church?**

A: One, holy, catholic, and apostolic.

In the Bible: Ephesians 2:20, 4:3, 5:26; Matthew 28:19; Revelation 21:14
In the *Catechism*: CCC, 813, 823, 830, 857

54. **Q: How does the Church preserve the teachings of Jesus?**

A: Through Sacred Scripture and Sacred Tradition.

In the Bible: 2 Timothy 2:2; 2 Thessalonians 2:15
In the *Catechism*: CCC, 78, 81, 82

55. **Q: How does the Church's calendar differ from the secular calendar?**

A: The first day of the Church's year is the first Sunday of Advent, not January 1. The Church's calendar revolves around the life, death, and Resurrection of Jesus. Throughout the course of the Church's year the whole mystery of Jesus Christ is unfolded.

In the Bible: Luke 2:1–20; 1 Corinthians 15:3–4
In the *Catechism*: CCC, 1163, 1171, 1194

Going Deeper

Over the course of the year, through the readings at Mass, the feast days, and holy days, we experience the story of Jesus. The Church's calendar does this to remind us that Jesus' story is not just about what happened over two thousand years ago. It is about our friendship with him today. The mystery of his life, teachings, and saving grace is unfolding in your life and the life of the Church today.

56. **Q: Did Jesus give special authority to one of the apostles?**

A: Yes, to Peter when Jesus said to him, "I will give you the keys of the kingdom of heaven, and whatever you bind on earth shall be bound in heaven, and whatever you loose on earth shall be loosed in heaven."

In the Bible: Mark 3:16, 9:2; Luke 24:34
In the *Catechism*: *CCC*, 552, 881

57. **Q: Who speaks with the authority that Jesus gave to St. Peter?**

A: The pope, who is St. Peter's successor, the bishop of Rome, and the vicar of Christ on earth.

In the Bible: Matthew 16:18; John 21:15–17
In the *Catechism*: CCC, 891

58. **Q: What is the name of the present pope?**

A: Pope Francis.

In the Bible: Matthew 16:18; John 21:15–17
In the *Catechism*: CCC, 936

59. **Q: What is the sacred liturgy?**

A: The Church's public worship of God.

In the Bible: John 4:23–24
In the *Catechism*: CCC, 1069, 1070

60. **Q: What attitude should we have when we participate in the sacred liturgy?**

A: We should have the attitude of reverence in our hearts and respect in our actions and appearance.

In the Bible: Hebrews 12:28
In the *Catechism*: CCC, 2097

61. **Q: What is a sacrament?**

A: A sacrament is an outward sign, instituted by Christ and entrusted to the Church to give grace. Grace bears fruit in those who receive them with the required dispositions.

In the Bible: 2 Peter 1:4
In the *Catechism*: CCC, 1131

Going Deeper

God gives you grace to help you do what is good and right. When you are open to God, he also gives you the grace to be kind, generous, courageous, and compassionate toward others. Grace

bears good fruit in our lives. One of the most powerful ways God shares his grace with us is through the sacraments. This grace helps us to become the-very-best-version-of-ourselves, grow in virtue, and live holy lives.

62. **Q: How does Jesus share his life with us?**

A: During his earthly life, Jesus shared his life with others through his words and actions; now he shares the very same life with us through the sacraments.

In the Bible: John 3:16; John 6:5–7
In the *Catechism*: CCC, 521, 1131, 1115–1116

Going Deeper

God loves to share his life and love with us. We can experience his life through daily prayer, Scripture, and through serving one another. The most powerful way that God shares his life with us is through the sacraments. Sunday Mass and regular reconciliation are two sacraments that guide us and encourage us on our journey to become the-best-version-of-ourselves, grow in virtue, and live holy lives.

63. **Q: How many sacraments are there?**

A: Seven.

> In the Bible: John 20:22–23; Luke 22:14–20; John 7:37–39; James 5:14–16; Hebrews 5:1–6; Matthew 19:6
> In the *Catechism*: CCC, 1113

64. **Q: What are the seven sacraments, and which ones have you received?**

A: Baptism, penance, Holy Eucharist, confirmation, holy orders, matrimony, anointing of the sick. You have received baptism, penance, and Holy Eucharist.

> In the Bible: John 20:22–23; Luke 22:14–20; John 7:37–39; James 5:14–16; Hebrews 5:1–6; Matthew 19:6
> In the *Catechism*: CCC, 1113

65. **Q: What are the sacraments you can only receive once?**

A: Baptism, confirmation, and holy orders.

> In the Bible: Ephesians 4:30
> In the *Catechism*: CCC, 1272

66. **Q: How is Christian initiation accomplished?**

A: Christian initiation is accomplished with three sacraments: baptism which is the beginning of new life; confirmation which strengthens our new life in Christ; and the Eucharist which nourishes the disciple with Jesus' Body and Blood so that we can be transformed in Christ.

> In the Bible: John 3:5; Acts 8:14–17; John 6:51–58
> In the *Catechism*: CCC, 1212, 1275

Going Deeper

Life is a journey with God. Baptism, confirmation and first Communion are all great moments in your journey. They are sacraments that work together to help you live your best life. In

baptism you receive new life in Jesus, in confirmation God reminds us that he has a special mission for each and every single one of us, and Holy Communion gives us the strength and the wisdom to live that mission by serving God and others.

67. Q: **When you were born, did you have sanctifying grace (a share in God's life)?**

A: No.

In the Bible: Colossians 1:12–14
In the *Catechism*: *CCC*, 403, 1250

68. Q: **Why are we not born with sanctifying grace?**

A: Because we are born with original sin, which is the loss of sanctifying grace.

In the Bible: Genesis 3:23
In the *Catechism*: *CCC*, 403, 1250

69. **Q: Was any human person conceived without original sin?**

A: Yes, Mary at her Immaculate Conception.

> In the Bible: Luke 1:28
> In the *Catechism*: CCC, 491, 492

70. **Q: What was the original sin?**

A: Adam and Eve were tempted by the devil, and they chose to distrust God's goodness and to disobey his law.

> In the Bible: Genesis 3:1–11; Romans 5:19
> In the *Catechism*: CCC, 397

71. **Q: Is there really a devil?**

A: Yes.

> In the Bible: 1 John 5:19; 1 Peter 5:8
> In the *Catechism*: CCC, 391

72. **Q: Is it easier to be bad or to be good?**

A: It is easier to be bad, because original sin has left us with an inclination to sin called concupiscence.

In the Bible: Romans 7:15–18
In the *Catechism*: CCC, 409, 1264, 2516

73. **Q: When did you receive sanctifying grace for the first time?**

A: At baptism.

In the Bible: 2 Corinthians 5:17
In the *Catechism*: CCC, 1265

74. **Q: What is baptism?**

A: Baptism is the sacrament of rebirth in Jesus that is necessary for salvation.

In the Bible: 2 Corinthians 5:17; 2 Peter 1:4; Galatians 4:5–7
In the *Catechism*: CCC, 1266, 1277, 1279

Going Deeper

Baptism is a great blessing. Through your baptism you became a member of the Catholic Church. This is another wonderful reason why being Catholic is a great blessing. Through your baptism, you received new life in Jesus. You were made for mission. God had that mission in mind when you were baptized, and every day since he has been preparing you for your mission. We discover that mission through prayer, the sacraments, and service to others. God doesn't reveal our mission all at once, he reveals it step by step.

75. **Q: What are the fruits of baptism?**

   A: Baptism makes us Christians, cleanses us of original sin and personal sin, and reminds us that we are children of God and members of the body of Christ—the Church.

   In the Bible: Galatians 4:5–7
   In the *Catechism*: CCC, 1279

Going Deeper

In baptism God gives us many gifts. We become Christian, our sins are forgiven, we are given new life in Jesus, and God marks us for a great mission. God is able to do this through the power of the Holy Spirit. In baptism our souls are flooded with the gift of the Holy Spirit, which helps us in our journey to grow closer to God. Each and every sacrament we receive is full of gifts, big and small. Every blessing reminds us that we are all sons and daughters of a loving Father.

76. **Q: What did baptism do for you?**

A: It gave me a share in God's life for the first time, made me a child of God, and took away original sin.

In the Bible: 2 Corinthians 5:17; 2 Peter 1:4; Galatians 4:5–7
In the *Catechism*: CCC, 1266, 1279

77. Q: How old does someone need to be to receive baptism?

A: A person can be baptized at any age. Since the earliest times of Christianity, baptism has been administered to infant children because baptism is a grace and a gift that is freely given by God and does not presuppose any human merit.

In the Bible: Acts 2:37–39
In the *Catechism*: CCC, 1282

Going Deeper

God's love is a free gift. There is nothing you could do to earn or lose God's love. You may be tempted to think that God's love is something to be earned. This is simply not true. God loved you into life, and God loved you into the Church. You did nothing to be born, and if you were baptized as an infant, you did nothing to be baptized. You didn't do anything to deserve life or baptism. God freely gives you life and faith.

78. **Q: Who administers the sacrament of baptism?**

A: Anyone can administer the sacrament of baptism in an emergency by pouring water over that person's head and saying, "I baptize you in the name of the Father, and of the Son, and of the Holy Spirit." Baptism, however, is usually administered by a priest or deacon.

In the Bible: Matthew 28:19
In the *Catechism*: CCC, 1284

Going Deeper

Not everyone is baptized as an infant. Some people don't learn about Jesus until they are adults. But God wants everyone to receive the blessing of baptism. He wants everyone to be a part of his family—the Catholic Church. He wants everyone to be free from original sin. He wants everyone to have new life in his Son, Jesus. He wants everyone to spend eternity with him in heaven.

79. Q: **How long do you remain a child of God?**

A: Forever.

> In the Bible: 1 Peter 1:3–4
> In the *Catechism*: *CCC*, 1272, 1274

80. Q: **Can you lose a share in God's life after baptism?**

A: Yes.

> In the Bible: Mark 3:29
> In the *Catechism*: *CCC*, 1861

81. Q: **Can we lose the new life of grace that God has freely given us?**

A: Yes. The new life of grace can be lost by sin.

> In the Bible: 1 Corinthians 6:9; 2 Corinthians 5:19–21; 1 John 1:9
> In the *Catechism*: *CCC*, 1420

Going Deeper

At baptism we are filled with a very special grace. This grace blesses us with new life and brings us into friendship with God. That new life can be hurt or lost when we sin. When that happens, don't worry because God has given us the blessing of reconciliation! As long as we are truly sorry for our sins and go to reconciliation, we can once again experience the fullness of life with God. Reconciliation is a great blessing!

82. **Q: How can you lose sanctifying grace (a share in God's life)?**
A: By committing mortal sin.

In the Bible: Galatians 5:19–21; Romans 1:28–32
In the *Catechism*: *CCC*, 1861

83. **Q: Which is the worse sin: venial or mortal?**
A: Mortal (deadly) sin.

In the Bible: 1 John 5:16
In the *Catechism*: *CCC*, 1855, 1874, 1875

84. **Q: What three things are necessary to commit a mortal sin?**
A: 1. You must disobey God in a serious matter.
2. You must know that it is wrong.
3. You must freely choose to do it anyway.

In the Bible: Mark 10:19; Luke 16:19–31; James 2:10–11
In the *Catechism: CCC*, 1857

85. **Q: What happens to you if you die in a state of mortal sin?**
A: You go to hell.

In the Bible: 1 John 3:14–15; Matthew 25:41–46
In the *Catechism: CCC*, 1035, 1472, 1861, 1874

86. **Q: Is there really a hell?**
A: Yes; it is the place of eternal separation from God.

In the Bible: Isaiah 66:24; Mark 9:47, 48
In the *Catechism: CCC*, 1035

87. **Q: What happens if you die with venial sin on your soul?**

A: You go to purgatory, where you are purified and made perfect.

In the Bible: 1 Corinthians 3:14–15; 2 Maccabees 12:45–46
In the *Catechism*: *CCC*, 1030, 1031, 1472

88. **Q: What happens to the souls in purgatory after their purification?**

A: They go to heaven.

In the Bible: 2 Maccabees 12:45
In the *Catechism*: *CCC*, 1030

89. **Q: Is there really a heaven?**

A: Yes; it is the place of eternal happiness with God.

In the Bible: 1 John 3:2; 1 Corinthians 13:12; Revelation 22:4–5
In the *Catechism*: *CCC*, 1023, 1024

90. **Q: Can any sin, no matter how serious, be forgiven?**

A: Yes, any sin, no matter how serious or how many times it is committed, can be forgiven.

In the Bible: Matthew 18:21–22
In the *Catechism*: *CCC*, 982

91. **Q: What is the primary purpose of the sacrament of reconciliation?**

A: The primary purpose of the sacrament of reconciliation is the forgiveness of sins committed after baptism.

In the Bible: Sirach 18:12–13; Sirach 21:1; Acts 26:17–18
In the *Catechism*: *CCC*, 1421, 1446, 1468

Going Deeper

Through baptism we become children of God, are welcomed into a life of grace, and are given the promise of heaven. As we get older, we may do things that harm our relationship with God. But God keeps loving us, and invites us to participate in regular reconciliation so that our friendship with him can always be as

strong as it was in baptism. If we offend God, the best thing to do is to say sorry to God by going to reconciliation.

92. **Q: What other names is the sacrament of reconciliation known by?**

A: In different places and different times, the sacrament of reconciliation is also called the sacrament of conversion, confession, or penance.

In the Bible: Mark 1:15; Proverbs 28:13; Acts 3:19; 2 Peter 3:9
In the *Catechism*: *CCC*, 1423, 1424

Going Deeper

Jesus loves you and he wants to save you from your sins. He wants to save you because he wants to live in friendship with you on earth and in heaven. He wants to share his joy with you and he wants you to share that joy with others. No matter what name is used, the sacrament of reconciliation restores our friendship with God and helps us become the-best-version-of-ourselves, grow in virtue, and live a holy life.

93. **Q: Is the sacrament of reconciliation a blessing?**

A: Yes, it is a great blessing from God.

In the Bible: Psalm 32:1–2; Romans 4:6–8
In the *Catechism*: CCC, 1468, 1496

94. **Q: Who commits sins?**

A: All people sin.

In the Bible: Romans 3:23–25; 1 John 1:8–10
In the *Catechism*: CCC, 827

95. **Q: How can a mortal sin be forgiven?**

A: Through the sacrament of reconciliation.

In the Bible: 2 Corinthians 5:20–21
In the *Catechism*: CCC, 1446, 1497

96. **Q: What is the ordinary way for someone to be reconciled with God and his Church?**

   A: The ordinary way for someone to be reconciled with God and his Church is by personally confessing all grave sin to a priest and then receiving absolution.

   In the Bible: John 20:23
   In the *Catechism: CCC*, 1497

   ## Going Deeper

   We all stray away from God from time to time. When we do, it is a good time to go to the sacrament of reconciliation and say sorry to God. You might be tempted to fall into the trap of thinking that your sin is too big for God to forgive. But, there is nothing you can do that will make God stop loving you. The doors of the Church are always open and God is always willing to forgive us when are sorry. The sacrament of reconciliation is a great blessing!

97. **Q: What three things must you do in order to receive forgiveness of sin in the sacrament of confession?**

A: 1. You must be truly sorry for your sins.

2. Confess all mortal sins in kind and number committed since your last confession.

3. You must resolve to amend your life.

In the Bible: Romans 8:17; Romans 3:23–26
In the *Catechism*: CCC, 1448

Going Deeper

When we sin we become restless and unhappy. God doesn't want us to be restless and unhappy so he invites us to come to reconciliation so that he can fill us with his joy. There may be times in your life when you feel far from God. But never think that God doesn't want you to return to him. Never think that your sins are greater than God's love. God's love and mercy will always be waiting for you in the sacrament of reconciliation.

98. **Q: What are the three actions required of us in the sacrament of reconciliation?**

A: The three actions required of us in the sacrament of reconciliation are repentance, confession of sins to the priest, and the intention to atone for our sins by performing the penance given by the priest.

In the Bible: 1 John 1:9
In the *Catechism*: *CCC*, 1491

Going Deeper

Regular reconciliation is one of the most powerful ways that God shares his grace and mercy with us. God asks us to be sorry for our sins, confess them out loud to a priest, and do an act of penance so that our friendship with God can be restored and strengthened. The more you go to reconciliation, the more you will come to realize the incredible power of God's grace and mercy in your life.

99. Q: **Who has the power to forgive sin?**

A: Jesus Christ through a Catholic priest.

In the Bible: John 20:23; 2 Corinthians 5:18
In the *Catechism*: *CCC*, 1461, 1493, 1495

100. Q: **Can the priest talk about your sins with other people?**

A: No. The priest must keep secret all sins confessed to him.

In the Bible: 2 Corinthians 5:18–19
In the *Catechism*: *CCC*, 1467

Going Deeper

If you are nervous about going to confession, it's OK. Being nervous is natural. Just know that the priest is there to help you. He will not think poorly of you because of your sins or tell anyone what they are. Instead, he will be happy that you went to confession. Remember, the priest is there to encourage you, extend God's love and mercy to you, and to help you grow in virtue.

101. **Q: What is the purpose of penance?**

A: After you have confessed your sins, the priest will propose penance for you to perform. The purpose of these acts of penance is to repair the harm caused by sin and to re-establish the habits of a disciple of Christ.

In the Bible: Luke 19:8; Acts 2:38
In the *Catechism: CCC*, 1459–1460

Going Deeper

Friendship is beautiful but it is also fragile. God gives us the sacrament of reconciliation to heal the pain caused by sin and to repair our friendship with him. When we do our penance we show God that we are truly sorry. Penance helps our souls get healthy again.

102. **Q: How often should you go to confession?**

A: You should go immediately if you are in a state of mortal sin; otherwise, it is recommended to go once a month because it is highly recommended to confess venial sins. Prior to confession you should carefully examine your conscience.

In the Bible: Acts 3:19; Luke 5:31–32; Jeremiah 31:19
In the *Catechism*: *CCC*, 1457, 1458

Going Deeper

God loves healthy relationships, and forgiveness is essential to having healthy relationships. Regularly going to God in the sacrament of reconciliation and asking for forgiveness is a powerful way to have a fabulous relationship with God. Many of the saints went to reconciliation every month, some even more often. They knew that going to confession was the only way to be reconciled to God. They also knew that nothing brought them more joy than having a strong friendship with Jesus.

103. **Q: Does the sacrament of reconciliation reconcile us only with God?**

A: No. The sacrament of reconciliation reconciles us with God and with the Church.

In the Bible: 1 Corinthians 12:26
In the *Catechism*: *CCC*, 1422, 1449, 1469

Going Deeper

God delights in his relationship with you, and he delights in your relationship with the Church. Sin makes your soul sick, it hurts other people, and it harms your relationship with God and the Church. When we go to confession, God forgives us and heals our soul. He also heals our relationship with him and with the Church through the sacrament of reconciliation.

104. **Q: How do we experience God's mercy?**

A: We experience God's mercy in the sacrament of reconciliation. We also experience God's mercy through the kindness, generosity, and compassion of other people. God's mercy always draws us closer to him. We can also be instruments of God's mercy by exercising the works of mercy with kindness, generosity, and compassion.

In the Bible: Luke 3:11; John 8:11
In the *Catechism*: *CCC*, 1422, 1449, 2447

Going Deeper

Sometimes when we do something that is wrong we may be tempted to think that God will not love us anymore. But that is never true. God will always love you because our God is a merciful God. God shows us his mercy by forgiving us, teaching us, and caring for our physical and spiritual needs, even when we don't deserve it. He shows us his mercy through the sacrament of reconciliation and through the loving actions of other people. God invites you to spread his mercy by forgiving others, praying for others, and caring for those in need.

105. **Q: Where in the church building is Jesus present in a special way?**
   A: In the tabernacle.

   In the Bible: Exodus 40:34; Luke 22:19
   In the *Catechism*: CCC, 1379

106. **Q: Who is the source of all blessings?**

A: God is the source of all blessings. In the Mass we praise and adore God the Father as the source of every blessing in creation. We also thank God the Father for sending us his Son. Most of all we express our gratitude to God the Father for making us his children.

In the Bible: Luke 1:68–79; Psalm 72:18–19
In the *Catechism*: *CCC*, 1083, 1110

Going Deeper

You are blessed in so many ways. But every blessing comes from the very first blessing—life! God has given you life and made you his child. This is an incredible blessing! One of the greatest ways we can show God our gratitude is by going to Mass. By showing up every Sunday and participating in Mass, you show God how thankful you are for everything he has done for you.

107. Q: True or false: When you receive Holy Communion, you receive a piece of bread that signifies, symbolizes, or represents Jesus.

A: False.

In the Bible: Matthew 26:26
In the *Catechism*: CCC, 1374, 1413

108. Q: What do you receive in Holy Communion?

A: The Body, Blood, soul, and divinity of Christ.

In the Bible: 1 Corinthians 11:24; John 6:54–55
In the *Catechism*: CCC, 1374, 1413

Going Deeper

Jesus is truly present in the Eucharist. It is not a symbol; it is Jesus. We receive all of Jesus in the Eucharist. Even the tiniest crumb that falls from the wafer contains all of Jesus. The bread and wine become Jesus at the moment of consecration. This is an incredible moment. In this moment Jesus comes among us once again. Every time you go to Mass, bread and wine are transformed into the Body and Blood of Jesus. You are blessed to be able to receive Jesus in the Eucharist.

109. **Q: What is transubstantiation?**

A: Transubstantiation is when the bread and wine become the Body and Blood of Jesus.

In the Bible: Matthew 26:26; Mark 14:22; Luke 22:19–20
In the *Catechism*: CCC, 1376

Going Deeper

God has the power to transform everyone and everything he comes in contact with. Every day, in every Catholic Church, during every Mass, God transforms ordinary bread and wine into the Body and Blood of Jesus Christ. After receiving Jesus in the Eucharist, many of the saints prayed that they would become what they had received. God answered their prayers and transformed their lives by helping them to live like Jesus. Just like with the saints, God can transform your life. Every time you receive Jesus in the Eucharist worthily, you can become a little more like him. Just like Jesus, you can love generously and serve powerfully everyone you meet.

110. **Q: When does the bread and wine change into the Body and Blood of Christ?**

A: It is changed by the words and intention of the priest at the moment of consecration during Mass. The priest, asking for the help of the Holy Spirit, says the same words Jesus said at the Last Supper: "This is my body which will be given up for you . . . This is the cup of my blood . . ."

In the Bible: Mark 14:22; Luke 22:19–20
In the *Catechism*: CCC, 1412, 1413

Going Deeper

The Last Supper is the most famous meal in the history of the world. In that room two thousand years ago, Jesus gave himself completely to his apostles. Every time we come to Mass, the priest recites the same words as Jesus during the Last Supper. When he does, the wheat bread and grape wine become the Body and Blood of Jesus. Amazing! Jesus wants to give himself completely to you just as he gave himself completely to his apostles at the Last Supper. Jesus wants to be invited into your life. He wants to encourage you, guide you, listen to you, and love you. He offers himself to you in a special way at Mass, especially in the amazing gift of Holy Communion.

111. **Q: What are the benefits of receiving the Body and Blood of Jesus in the Eucharist?**

A: When you receive Jesus in the Eucharist, you become more united with the Lord, your venial sins are forgiven, and you are given grace to avoid grave sins. Receiving Jesus in the Eucharist also increases your love for Jesus and reinforces the fact that you are a member of God's family—the Catholic Church.

In the Bible: John 6:56–57
In the *Catechism*: *CCC*, 1391–1396

Going Deeper
The Eucharist empowers us to do great things for God. The saints did incredible things for God throughout their lives and the Eucharist was the source of their strength. Through Holy

Communion we grow closer to God, move further away from sinful habits, and grow in love for Jesus and the Catholic Church. The Eucharist is the ultimate food for your soul, and it will give you the strength and courage to serve God and others powerfully just like the saints.

112. **Q: How important is the Eucharist to the life of the Church?**

A: The Eucharist is indispensable in the life of the Church. The Eucharist is the heart of the Church. One of the reasons the Eucharist is so important to the life of the Church is because, through it, Jesus unites every member of the Church with his sacrifice on the cross. Every grace that flows from Jesus' suffering, death, and Resurrection comes to us through the Church.

In the Bible: John 6:51, 54, 56
In the *Catechism: CCC*, 1324, 1331, 1368, 1407

Going Deeper

Jesus promised to be with us always, no matter what. He has been keeping this promise for over 2,000 years. Jesus is always with us in the Eucharist. The Eucharist unites us to Jesus and his Church. It also unites us to one another. We are blessed to have the Eucharist. Only through the Catholic Church can we receive the gift of the Eucharist. We are blessed to be Catholic.

113. **Q: Should you receive Holy Communion in the state of mortal sin?**
  A: No. If you do, you commit the additional mortal sin of sacrilege.

In the Bible: 1 Corinthians 11:27–29
In the *Catechism*: CCC, 1385, 1415, 1457

Going Deeper

If Jesus came to visit your home and it was so messy you couldn't open the door to let Jesus in, that would be terrible. No matter how much Jesus wants to be a part of our lives he will never force himself upon us. Mortal sin slams the door of our souls in Jesus' face. It breaks our relationship with God and prevents the wonderful graces of the Eucharist from flowing into our hearts, minds, and souls. Reconciliation reopens the door to our souls and lets Jesus enter our lives again.

114. **Q: What is sacrilege?**

A: It is the abuse of a sacred person, place, or thing.

In the Bible: 1 Corinthians 11:27–29
In the *Catechism*: CCC, 2120

115. **Q: If you are in a state of mortal sin, what should you do before receiving Holy Communion?**

A: You should go to confession as soon as possible.

In the Bible: 2 Corinthians 5:20
In the *Catechism*: CCC, 1385, 1457

116. **Q: Who offered the first Mass?**

A: Jesus Christ.

In the Bible: Mark 14:22–24
In the *Catechism*: CCC, 1323

117. **Q: When did Jesus offer the first Mass?**

A: On Holy Thursday night, the night before he died, at the Last Supper.

In the Bible: Matthew 26:26–28
In the *Catechism*: CCC, 1323

118. **Q: Who offers the Eucharistic sacrifice?**

A: Jesus is the eternal high priest. In the Mass, he offers the Eucharistic sacrifice through the ministry of the priest.

In the Bible: Mark 14:22; Matthew 26:26; Luke 22:19; 1 Corinthians 11:24
In the *Catechism*: CCC, 1348

Going Deeper

The Last Supper was the first Eucharistic celebration. This was the apostles' first Communion, and the first time anybody had ever received the Eucharist. The Mass is not just a symbol of what happened that night. Jesus is truly present in the Eucharist. Every time we receive Holy Communion Jesus gives himself to us in the same way he gave himself to his apostles over 2,000 years ago. Jesus works through the priest at Mass to transform the bread and wine into his Body and Blood.

119. **Q: What is the Sacrifice of the Mass?**

A: It is the sacrifice of Jesus Christ on Calvary, the memorial of Christ's Passover, made present when the priest repeats the words of consecration spoken by Jesus over the bread and wine at the Last Supper.

In the Bible: Hebrews 7:25–27
In the *Catechism: CCC*, 1364, 1413

Going Deeper

God loves you so much, and he will go to unimaginable lengths to prove his love for you. On Good Friday Jesus was beaten, bullied, mocked, spat upon, cursed at, and crucified on the cross. Jesus laid down his life for us. On Easter Sunday Jesus rose from the dead. He did this so that we might live a very different life while here on earth and happily with him forever in heaven. Every time we go to Mass we remember the life of Jesus, the path he invites us to walk, and the incredible lengths to which he went to show us his love.

120. **Q: Who can preside at the Eucharist?**

A: Only an ordained priest can preside at the Eucharist and consecrate the bread and the wine so that they become the Body and Blood of Jesus.

In the Bible: John 13:3–8
In the *Catechism*: CCC, 1411

Going Deeper

To be a priest is a great honor and privilege. Priests lay down their lives to serve God and his people. The priesthood is a life of service. One of the ultimate privileges of the priesthood is standing in Jesus' place and transforming bread and wine into the Eucharist. This privilege is reserved for priests alone. Nobody other than a priest can do this.

121. **Q: How do we participate in the Sacrifice of the Mass?**

A: By uniting ourselves and our intentions to the bread and wine, offered by the priest, which become Jesus' sacrifice to the Father.

In the Bible: Romans 12:1
In the *Catechism*: CCC, 1407

122. **Q: What does the Eucharistic celebration we participate in at Mass always include?**

A: The Eucharist celebration always includes the proclamation of the Word of God, thanksgiving to God the Father for all his blessings, the consecration of the bread and wine, and participation in the liturgical banquet by receiving the Lord's Body and Blood. These elements constitute one single act of worship.

In the Bible: Luke 24:13–35
In the *Catechism*: CCC, 1345–1355, 1408

Going Deeper

The Mass follows a certain formula that is always repeated and never changes. You could go to Mass anywhere in the world and you would always find it is the same. At every Mass we read from the Bible, show God our gratitude for the blessing of Jesus, witness bread and wine transformed into the Body and Blood of Jesus, and receive Jesus during Holy Communion. In the midst of this great routine, God wants to surprise you. You could spend a lifetime going to Mass every single day and at the end of your life still be surprised by what God has to say to you in the Mass. The Mass is truly amazing!

123. **Q: What role does music play in the Mass?**
A: Sacred music helps us to worship God.

In the Bible: Psalm 57:8–10; Ephesians 5:19; Hebrews 2:12; Colossians 3:16
In the *Catechism*: CCC, 1156

Going Deeper
Sometimes when we are praying it can be difficult to find the right words to express how we feel. To help us, God gives us the great gift of sacred music. Over the course of the Mass there will be songs of praise, songs of worship, songs of petition, and songs of

thanksgiving. Sacred music helps raise our hearts to God and bond us together as a community calling out to God with one voice.

124. **Q: What is the Lord's Day?**

A: Sunday is the Lord's Day. It is a day of rest. It is a day to gather as a family. It is the principal day for celebrating the Eucharist because it is the day of the Resurrection.

In the Bible: Exodus 31:15; Matthew 28:1; Mark 16:2; John 20:1
In the *Catechism*: CCC, 1166, 1193, 2174

Going Deeper

Sunday is a very special day. The Resurrection of Jesus is so important that we celebrate it every day at Mass. But we celebrate the Resurrection of Jesus in a special way every Sunday. We do that by resting, spending time with family, and going to Mass. The Lord's Day is a day to marvel at all the amazing ways God has blessed us, and because of that it is a day of gratitude.

125. **Q: Is it a mortal sin for you to miss Mass on Sunday or a holy day through your own fault?**

A: Yes.

> In the Bible: Exodus 20:8
> In the *Catechism*: *CCC*, 2181

126. **Q: Which Person of the Holy Trinity do you receive in confirmation?**

A: The Holy Spirit.

> In the Bible: Romans 8:15
> In the *Catechism*: *CCC*, 1302

127. **Q: What happens in the sacrament of confirmation?**

A: The Holy Spirit comes upon us and strengthens us to be soldiers of Christ, that we may spread and defend the Catholic faith.

> In the Bible: John 14:26; 15:26
> In the *Catechism*: *CCC*, 1303, 2044

128. **Q: What is confirmation?**

A: Confirmation is a sacrament that perfects baptismal grace. Through it we receive the Holy Spirit and are strengthened in grace so we can grow in virtue, live holy lives, and carry out the mission God calls us to.

In the Bible: John 20:22; Acts 2:1–4
In the *Catechism*: CCC, 1285, 1316

Going Deeper

When you are older you will be blessed to receive the sacrament of confirmation. Confirmation reminds us that in baptism God blessed us with a special mission and filled us with the Holy Spirit. Through an outpouring of the Holy Spirit at confirmation, we are filled with the courage and wisdom to live out the mission God has given us. Confirmation deepens our friendship with Jesus and the Catholic Church. It reminds us that we are sons and daughters of a great King. It will be a special moment in your life and a wonderful blessing!

129. Q: **When is confirmation received?**

A: Most Catholics in the West receive confirmation during their teenage years, but in the East confirmation is administered immediately after baptism.

In the Bible: Hebrews 6:1–3
In the *Catechism*: *CCC*, 1306, 1318

Going Deeper

Baptism, confirmation, and first Holy Communion are called the sacraments of initiation. In a special way, the sacraments of initiation deepen our friendship with Jesus and the Church, fill us with what we need to live out God's mission for our lives, and inspire us to become all that God created us to be. It is important to remember that these three sacraments are connected. They are the foundation for a fabulous friendship with God on earth and forever in heaven. In some parts of the world, and at different times throughout history, people have received these sacraments at different times according to local traditions and practical

considerations. For example, hundreds of years ago, the bishop may have only visited a village once every two or three years, and so confirmation would take place when he visited. Even today, some children receive baptism, first Communion, and confirmation all at the same time.

130. Q: **What are the seven gifts of the Holy Spirit?**
A: Wisdom, understanding, counsel, fortitude, knowledge, piety, and fear of the Lord.

In the Bible: Isaiah 11:2–3
In the *Catechism*: *CCC*, 1830, 1831

131. Q: **Before you are confirmed, you will promise the bishop that you will never give up the practice of your Catholic faith for anyone or anything. Did you ever make that promise before?**
A: Yes, at baptism.

In the Bible: Joshua 24:21–22
In the *Catechism*: *CCC*, 1298

132. **Q: Most of you were baptized as little babies. How could you make that promise?**

A: Our parents and godparents made that promise for us.

In the Bible: Mark 16:16
In the *Catechism*: *CCC*, 1253

133. **Q: What kind of sin is it to receive confirmation in the state of mortal sin?**

A: A sacrilege.

In the Bible: 1 Corinthians 11:27–29
In the *Catechism*: *CCC*, 2120

134. **Q: If you have committed mortal sin, what should you do before receiving confirmation?**

A: You should make a good confession.

In the Bible: 2 Corinthians 5:20; Luke 15:18
In the *Catechism*: *CCC*, 1310

135. **Q: What are the three traditional vocations?**

A: Married life, holy orders, and the consecrated life.

> In the Bible: Ephesians 5:31–32; Hebrews 5:6, 7:11; Psalm 110:4; Matthew 19:12; 1 Corinthians 7:34–66
> In the *Catechism*: CCC, 914, 1536, 1601

136. **Q: What are the three vows that a consecrated man or woman takes?**

A: Chastity, poverty, and obedience.

> In the Bible: Matthew 19:21; Matthew 19:12; 1 Corinthians 7:34–36; Hebrews 10:7
> In the *Catechism*: CCC, 915

137. **Q: What are the three ranks (degrees) of holy orders?**

A: Deacon, priest, and bishop.

> In the Bible: 1 Timothy 4:14; 2 Timothy 1:6–7
> In the *Catechism*: CCC, 1554

138. **Q: For whom did God make marriage?**

A: One man and one woman.

> In the Bible: Genesis 1:26–28; Ephesians 5:31
> In the *Catechism*: *CCC*, 1601, 2360

139. **Q: Is it possible for two men or two women to get married?**

A: No.

> In the Bible: Genesis 19:1–29; Romans 1:24–27; 1 Corinthians 6:9
> In the *Catechism*: *CCC*, 2357, 2360

140. **Q: When can a man and woman begin living together?**

A: Only after their marriage.

> In the Bible: 1 Corinthians 6:18–20
> In the *Catechism*: *CCC*, 235

141. **Q: What are the three marriage promises a husband and wife make to each other?**

A: Faithfulness, permanence, and openness to having children.

In the Bible: Matthew 19:6; Genesis 1:28
In the *Catechism*: CCC, 1640, 1641, 1664

142. **Q: Why is abortion wrong?**

A: Because it takes the life of a baby in its mother's womb.

In the Bible: Jeremiah 1:5; Psalm 139:13
In the *Catechism*: CCC, 2270

143. **Q: How many commandments are there?**

A: Ten.

In the Bible: Exodus 20:1–18; Deuteronomy 5:6–21
In the *Catechism*: CCC, 2054

144. Q: What are the Ten Commandments?

A: 1. 1, the Lord, am your God. You shall not have other gods besides me.

2. You shall not take the name of the Lord, your God, in vain.

3. Remember to keep holy the Lord's Day.

4. Honor your father and mother.

5. You shall not kill.

6. You shall not commit adultery.

7. You shall not steal.

8. You shall not bear false witness against your neighbor.

9. You shall not covet your neighbor's wife.

10. You shall not covet your neighbor's goods.

In the Bible: Exodus 20:1–18; Deuteronomy 5:6–21
In the *Catechism*: CCC, 496, 497

145. **Q: What are the four main kinds of prayer?**

A: The four main kinds of prayer are adoration, thanksgiving, petition, and intercession.

In the Bible: Psalm 95:6; Colossians 4:2; James 5:16; 1 John 3:22
In the *Catechism: CCC*, 2628, 2629, 2634, 2638, 2639

146. **Q: How often should we pray?**

A: Every day.

In the Bible: 1 Thessalonians 5:17; Luke 18:1
In the *Catechism: CCC*, 2742

NOTES

NOTES

NOTES

NOTES

NOTES

NOTES

My Little Catechism

©2018 The Dynamic Catholic Institute and Kakadu, LLC.
Published by Wellspring

Illustrations by Carolina Farias
Design by The Dynamic Catholic Design Team

ISBN: 978-1-63582-039-3 (softcover)

For more information on this title or other books and CDs available through the Dynamic Catholic Book Program, please visit: www.DynamicCatholic.com.

The Dynamic Catholic Institute
5081 Olympic Blvd
Erlanger, Kentucky 41018
Phone: 1-859-980-7900
Email: info@DynamicCatholic.com

FIRST EDITION

10   9   8   7   6   5   4   3   2

Printed in the United States of America